Crush

And Other Love Poems For Girls

Jodie Toohey

**Wordsy Woman
Press**

Crush
And Other Love Poems for Girls
All Rights Reserved.
Copyright © 2015 Jodie Toohey V3.0

ISBN: 0692344497
ISBN-13: 978-0692344491 (Wordsy Woman Press)

DEDICATION

This book is dedicated to all those who have loved, lost, and gotten over it. Keep your hearts open.

Special thanks to readers of the first edition and everyone who's supported me on this journey to author.

Table of Contents

ACKNOWLEDGMENTS

I Walk Here, Let Me In, and *With Me* also appear in the *Other Side of Crazy* poetry collection by Jodie Toohey published by 918studio (918studio.net) in 2013.

Orphan is new to this edition and has never been published.

i

Chapter 1
The Crush

Jodie Toohey

Crush

When my eyes close at night,
Always there he is;
Those big blue eyes
And lips I want to kiss.

He's always right there
When dreams start to play;
Always holding my hand
Gazing at me the love-way.

The dream always ends
With words he must share;
Always I'm the only one;
Only girl for whom he cares.

Just as his lips lean
To my cheek for a kiss,
My alarm always rings,
Left with elusive bliss.

Though I'm awake,
The image will stay.
As I eat my cheerios,
I hope today is the day.

When I get to my locker,
He'll be waiting there.

Crush

He'll say "Where've you been?"
"I've looked everywhere."

He'll say he's been blind;
That's what it is.
He'll place his hand over mine
And promise I'll always be his.

Jodie Toohey

Wall Of Diversion

Your face is haunting my mind
Pushing away all other thoughts.
As each day passes I find myself
Dreaming of you more as I sense
You dream of me.
But a wall blocks us
From attempting more
Than this friendship we have
Which depends on others.
The wall is two people:
The woman you go out with
But say you hate
And the man I care about
Who's away but can still be hurt;
A man who's returning.
So what do we do?
Do we stay these friends
And lose a chance for true love,
Or risk our blooming friendship
By allowing our eyes to meet too much
And tearing down the wall
Then break up as all seem to
And be left with nothing?
Or do we do as we have been:
Sneaking glances and brushes
That no one else shares?
Waiting for a sign
That will assure us it's okay;
We can give in to our feelings
And it will be worth the risk?

Mirror Of My Soul

I look deep into your eyes
But don't know what I see.
Your eyes don't look away;
Can they see inside of me?

Can you hear me forcing my heart
To push out feelings creeping in?
Do you watch my inner battle,
Wondering if the fight my heart will win?

Can you feel my body tense
As I refrain from hugging you?
Can you see my hands thinking,
Trying to find something to do?

Do you see the image of your face
Fixed in front of my eyes?
Do you know risk I long to take'?
Do you hear my muffled cries?

Do you hear my silent pleas
For you to give me a sign?
Pleas that want to know,
Are your eyes a mirror of mine?

Jodie Toohey

Change Of Heart

Sometimes I want you forever
And sometimes to let go.
Sometimes I start to say, "I love you,"
But then I just say, "No."

When you smile at me
My world is more than fine.
When you laugh and talk with me,
You make my spirit shine.

But when you look right past me
It darkens my whole life.
When you don't talk to me
You cut me like a knife.

Sometimes I let go and be happy;
Sometimes I fall apart.
But almost every time I see you,
I have a change of heart.

Crush

Do You?

Do you ever wish we were different,
Then hope we never change?
Sometimes when we're together,
Does your heart feel a bit strange?

Sometimes when you're sleeping,
Do you find me in your dreams?
And when bright sun starts your day,
The dream lingers, it seems?

Do you ever wonder
How we've become so close today,
And the time we were strangers
Seems so very far away?

When we're walking together,
Do you yearn to place your hand in mine?
Do you ever start to explain
But the words you cannot find?

Do you wonder if our friendship will end
Or if it will transform to something new?
Do you wish I was there when we're apart?
Do you have any of these feelings? I do.

Jodie Toohey

If I Knew

If you were here
And I knew,
I know what
I would do.
If I knew
You felt the same.
If I knew
We'd win the game.
If I knew
It would never end.
If I knew
You'd stay my friend,
I'd hold you tight
In my arms.
I'd try to experience
All of your charms.
I'd tell you, "I love you"
And have no fear,
And remain this way
For many years.

The Path I'll Take

I have my plans all laid out,
I know which way to go.
I have three years until I complete;
Three years until you know.

I have my path all figured out,
I know what I will do.
I will do everything it takes
To make my dreams come true.

My mission starts early this fall.
You're meant for me, I'll show.
I'll allow for everything,
Even for us to grow.

I'll make sure I have extra routes
For when you throw a curve.
I'll always leave myself an out,
So I won't have to swerve.

It'll be a long and trying trip,
But I know what is to be.
So, without even knowing it,
You'll fall in love with me.

Jodie Toohey

The Wall

I've built a wall
Through the years
As a fortress for my heart
And to lock away my fears.

This wall I've built
Keeps what I feel inside.
The bricks keep hurt away
So my tears have dried.

I cannot truly love anyone
Or fully give my heart away.
There's so much in my heart
To you I cannot say.

I try to understand
Because you asked me to.
I try to let my feelings show
But this wall won't let them through.

So please be patient
And aim for my heart
And maybe little by little
This wall will fall apart.

Hearts Alive

Just draw a heart,
Start at the base.
Go in one stroke,
Do not erase.
Drawing a heart
In this way
Is just like life
Day by day.
The first part is easy,
The pace is fast.
Then hit a hump
And the easy is past.
The last line of the first side
Is just a brief crisis,
So time you bide.
Now, then you go
Up a nice slope,
This is the high point;
You're full of hope.
The very last stroke,
Is easy going,
This is when now
Short this chapter's growing.
Now heart is drawn,
End meets beginning.
Start the journey all over
And another chapter start living.

Jodie Toohey

Secret Admirer

I don't have enough nerve
To say what's in my heart.
So this lack of confidence
Keeps you the missing part.

I'd pay a million dollars
Just to gaze into your eyes.
I will never treat you wrong,
And I'll never tell you lies.

Until I find the right moment,
I'll be on the outside looking in.
I'll be your secret admirer
Until, your heart, I win.

Illusions

I see you standing there
So I feel okay.
I see your gentle, smiling face,
But then it fades away.

You are in the distance
Calling out my name.
I call you, then realize,
You're only in the frame.

We make plans for our wedding,
Together, as a team.
When I reach for my wedding band,
I wake up from a dream.

All I have now are illusions,
But someday, you'll come true.
Someday, you'll be reality;
Someday you'll love me, too.

Jodie Toohey

Too Much

Too simple.
The words are
Too simple
To describe
What lives inside.
Maybe.
So much.
Forever.
And always.
To you.
To your face.
To your heart
That beats
Inside the dream.
The joy.
The luck.
The amazement.
The beauty.
And the life.
The good.
The bad.
The pain.
The fun.
The depth of
What lies beyond
The meaning of words.
Tomorrow.
And today.
Yesterday.
All of everything.
Anyway.
Somehow.

Defeat

Time ticks away
In silence
As you weigh heavy
On my heart.
How do we know
Which way to turn?
How do we know
Which bridges to burn?
How do we know
What's good or bad?
How do we know
What's happy or sad?

Jodie Toohey

You're The Only One

You're the only one I see
When my eyes close at night.
You're the only one I want
To make me feel all right.
You're the only one who understands
What my future means to me.
You're the only one I will let
Glimpse in my heart what others can't see.
You're the only one I want
To know me like no one else can.
You're the only one who can
Love me like no other man.
You're the only one I trust
With all my hopes, dreams, and fears.
You're the only one who'll ever
Hold the power to stop these tears.
You're the only one I love
Enough to make a life vow.
I only hope you understand this
Someday somehow.

Infinity

All languages of the world
Do not contain enough words
To describe how I feel
About you.
All the emptiness of space
Could not symbolize
The hole my life would have
Without you.
The tallest mountain on Earth
Could not rise to meet
The height of importance you
Amount to.

Jodie Toohey

Letters

Words never written,
Words never said.
Words never given;
Words never read.
Words dancing
Around my head.

How

How do you say goodbye?
When I look at you
I see a promise of
Tomorrow and a dream
To call my own
And share with you.
You have shown me beauty
Always around me
But never noticed.
So many beautiful memories
You have given to me.
So much feeling inside;
So many things I wish I had
So I could give them all to you.
I sit here next to you
As summer rain falls softly
Around us,
And I long to express
All that churns inside
But I don't.
Where do I find words
To fit the rhyme?
How do I find a way
To capture time?
Where do I roam
To find a place to fly?
Where do I wander
To find strength
To reach the sky?

Jodie Toohey

What Would You Say

What would you say
If I told you, "I love you?"
What would you say
If I told you I lied?
Told you I can let go of you,
While, inside, I cried?

What would you say
If I told you how I really feel,
But then said I want more than anything
To just be a friend?
What would you do?
Would you wonder if it will ever end?

What would you say
If I told you what I really want?
What would you say
If I told you I want back the friend I had
And the memories I have of you
That should make me happy, make me sad?

What would you say
If I told you these things?
Would it warm your heart,
Or send through it, a chill?
What would you say?
I don't know and never will.

Chapter 2
The Relationship

Jodie Toohey

Can

I cannot know what tomorrow
Will bring.
I cannot promise a song to sing.
I cannot give you
The moon and the stars.
I cannot heal all your wounds
Or fade all the scars.
I cannot give you
The world on a platter.
I cannot lie
With it doesn't matter.
I cannot walk away from you,
Though I fear I cannot stay.
I cannot promise you anything;
I cannot wipe the pain away.

I can open myself to you
And allow love to grow.
I can hold you in my heart
Wherever I may go.
I can think about you
Every second of the day.
I can hold you close
And wipe your tears away.
I can hold your smile
In my hands.
I can rest my cheek against your chest

And turn as in a dance.
I can kiss your lips
And set your spirit free.
I can promise you my love;
I can believe in you and me.

Jodie Toohey

Fairy Tale

A little girl dream
Of satin and lace.
Blue eyes dancing;
A beautiful face.

A dream of a life
Of love and happiness.
Soft kiss from our lips;
Strength in your caress.

A life we can share
Of you and me forever.
Warm touch from your skin;
A life for us together.

Share our love and life;
My little girl dream is real.
Love caresses warm lips;
My dream's no more surreal.

My Love, Our Love

My love, you are my favorite thing.
My love, beautiful music, we will sing.
My love, my trouble you have seen me through.
My love, I'll help you through your troubles too.
My love, you fill my life with joy.
My love, you forget when I so annoy.
My love, what feelings I have felt!
My love, I am ecstatic with the love we have built.
My love, my life I will share with you.
My love, love forever is what we will do.
My love, I am ready to love and to cherish.
My love, our love, I'm sure will not perish.
My love, with this ring I will be wed.
My love, we'll be married when all this is said.
My love, you are my husband and I am your wife.
My love, I am ready to live a wonderful life.

Jodie Toohey

Little Girl

A little girl
Blanketed with books
And words
Grew in solitude.

She once ran
Down a graveled
Winding road,
Speeding toward her future.

She silently cried
With the rain
Alone at night.

This little girl
Lived in her dreams
And in the illusion
Born to her thoughts.

The little girl
Lived here not long ago
Lost in a life
And in a reality
She never imagined.

Say It

Say it with prose;
Say it with rhyme.
Say it with a letter;
Say it with time.
Say you care;
Say you know.
Say you understand;
Say you won't go.
Say it without words
By touching my face.
Say your feelings
Will not erase.
Say it even if
You don't know where to start.
Say it any way you can,
But say it from your heart.

Jodie Toohey

On Top

The mountains in the distance;
Each one just as high,
Both are steep and rocky;
Climbing to the sky.

You choose a mountain
And I'll choose another.
We'll each run to them,
Separately together.

You climb your mountain
And I will climb mine.
Climb to the top
And watch the sun shine.

It may be a slow trip
But don't ever stop,
It may be awhile
But I'll see you on top.

When I Look
Into Your Eyes

It happened suddenly
With just a word or two.
Just a few phrases to me
To make me fall for you.

You took me by surprise
When you looked into my eyes
And told me that you care
And would always be there.

You made me forget
The ones I loved before
And I have to admit,
I'm walking through that door.

My feelings for you rise
When I look into your eyes
Because you're not afraid to tell me
Or to make me see.

No one's ever told me anything
Like you've told me now
And no one's ever made me sing
The songs I sing right now.

Jodie Toohey

You've never told me lies
Because when I looked into your eyes
I could see something there
That I haven't seen anywhere.
I want you to give this thing a try.
I want to stand with you.
Because I know I'll never cry
As long as I'm with you.

My heart lets out a sigh
When I look into your eyes
Because I see what is there
Is that you really care.

So this poem is to tell you
That my feelings have changed.
Now I have feelings that are new
And I've got these all arranged.

A little of me shies
When I look into your eyes
Because I saw something there
I've never seen anywhere.

Yes, we'll make history
And you'll be in my heart
And it's no mystery that
We'll never be apart.

Separation

You talked to me;
I fell for you.
Now I don't know
What to do.

You were there,
He was gone.
I never thought
I could be wrong.

Maybe you just
Remind me of him;
Or maybe I just
Need a friend.

He has my heart;
He won't give it back.
But I think you have
All that he lacks.

So why can't I
Give you my heart?
Why does my past
Keep us apart?

I hope you don't see
What I don't show.
Maybe someday he'll be gone;
I don't know.

Jodie Toohey

Follow

I'll never follow in your footsteps
Or ask you to follow in mine,
But as you walk along the road,
I will travel beside you.
I'll never stop walking on
When you slow your pace.
I'll never run to catch up
When you fly ahead.
But if you fall, I'll be right there
To pick you up and push you on.

Love Is...

Love is great,
Love is true,
Love is me,
Love is you.
Love can be
Sweeter than
Candy when
You give it to
Someone who
Loves you too.

Jodie Toohey

Tears

Wet is his laughter
So gentle, so bright.
So full of joy
That love is so right.
Warm is his skin
On which his tears fall,
And dry is his cheek
After to him, she calls.

My Dream

I have a dream.
I have not an
Ordinary dream.
I have a dream
To see the cities
Of my beautiful,
Wondrous world.
I have a dream
To share the world
With you, my love.
To show it to you
Through my eyes.
To see the cities
Springing up
In their amazing
Wondrous ways.
I have a dream
To share all my
Moments with you
And to see my world
Through your eyes.

Jodie Toohey

Where

Where did it start?
Where will it end?
When will it be over;
When did it begin?
At what moment
Did it happen?
At what moment
Did we know?
Did we always know
Where it would go?
Was fate aware of
What time would show?

Friends

Friends are we,
Friends we'll be,
Together, you and me.

We'll be friends forever,
Our friendship will never fade.
It will never fade, I'm sure.

I have full trust in you
And when I'm blue
I know you'll see me through.

We do each other favors
And I always savor
The time we spend together.

I have a good friend in you
You will always be my friend
And I'll always be yours, too.

Jodie Toohey

Escape

Tear drops to the water,
Face flows far away.
Unaware where to go
Or what to do today.

But forever I will hold you,
As forever we will learn.
We will travel together
And leave our fears to burn.

Chapter 3
The Goodbye

Jodie Toohey

Misconceptions

Things aren't always what they seem to be.
I can see that every time you look at me.

I thought you were kind, I thought you were the one.
I found out I was wrong so my happiness was done.

I know you didn't love me, but I thought at least you cared.
But now I know I was wrong; my feelings weren't shared.

Out of all the boys I knew, you meant the most to me.
And though you're gone now, in my heart is where you'll always be.

Why Is It?

Why is it now
When I look into your eyes,
My heart aches
And I feel so much?
Why is it now
I long to have your hand in mine
And your lips
Soft and gentle on my cheek?
Why is it now
I feel so much toward you
And emotionally bonded to you?
When yesterday
And the time I had your arms
And your lips
Soft and gentle
Is gone?

Francisco

August 28:

> He exposed his home
> With every word.

September 20:

> I laughed at the irony
> When I invited him to be
> My homecoming date.

> "Noh!!," Horrified;
> As if I had asked him
> To rob a bank.

> Language barrier.

December 14:

> He watched me dance
> And thought of me.

> "I wished I had not said, 'No'"
> We danced slow
> On the wooden gym floor.

Crush

February 14:

> He forgot the corsage
> But sweetly held my hand
> As he picked our paper rose
> And placed it in my hair.

March 6:

> He desired crazy memories.
> I took him to the dugout
> In cold pouring rain.
>
> We drank sparkling water
> By a tea-light candle,
> And danced to music
> We heard in our hearts.

March 30:

> I told him I loved him
> On the Mississippi bank.
> He worried, "Where can we go?"

May 13:

> He missed the senior prom;
> I would be there.
>
> It reminded him of going home
> And leaving the most important

Person in America behind.

June 6:

    His face crinkled in pain
    As we said goodbye
    And I left him
    Standing on the curb.

        I never asked the names
        Of his family.
        I read in our yearbook
        He loved to surf on the ocean.

March 22:

    One postcard;
    An aerial view of Vigo;
    No words from him,
    My name and address;
    Nothing more.

Lost

Memories sweet as
Candy.
Tears hot like fire.
Smiles bright as
Noon-time summer
Sun.
Beauty every moment.
Love every touch.
Loss and strength
In every teardrop.
Crying through pain
And anger;
Words cannot take
The day away.
Change attacked.
Souls soaring
Side by side.
Everything upon this world.
I lost you.

Jodie Toohey

All The Way To Spain

I send my thoughts across the sea
All the way to Spain.
To the man who stole my heart and took it
All the way to Spain.
Will he ever come to me across the sea
All the way from Spain?
I felt his heart breaking as he flew
All the way to Spain.
Through letters, I will send my love
All the way to Spain.
My heart will now always live across the sea,
All the way in Spain.

Even Though

Though I hardly see you
And we don't talk at all;
Even though love is gone;
Even though we took a fall;
Even though we made mistakes,
And made it disappear;
Even though you've hurt me so;
One thing, to me, is clear.
Even though I know it's wrong,
I don't know what to do.
Even though I wish it wasn't,
My heart is stuck with you.

Jodie Toohey

Endless Nights

As sleep stays far from my eyes,
I lie patiently to await the dawn.
As the moon crawls across the sky,
It's been another day again you're gone.

The stars twinkling over my head
Have been shining on you the same.
Night images flood my bed;
Mocking my role in this game.

I wonder what you do
In your existence so far away.
Does the sun gleam for you?
For my tomorrow is your today.

Does my face graze your brain?
Do you allow it long to stay?
Ever does it cause your eyes to rain?
Or invent a hope we meet again someday?

Does ever sleep neglect your soul?
So you await daybreak to bring tomorrow?
Do all the night, you turn, toss, and roll;
Praying light of day will abduct your sorrow?

Goodbye

Brush away the drops
Falling softly
Over my skin.
Silenced words
I should not speak
With a word escaping
Betraying lips.
Whisper your
Unspoken goodbye.

Jodie Toohey

Retort

I have not missed
The tears that fall
Every time you say you will,
Then don't.
I have not missed
Your empty words.
You value others' smiles
More than you value
Your own.
You know I do not,
So you believe that means
It's easy to smile alone,
At pain, at nothing.
I thought you knew me
More than you really did.
My greatest virtue is myself
And the rules I choose
To live by.
You value me,
But not enough to fight me.
You would rather give me
What I say I want
Than to fight to keep
What you want and value.
You are no martyr.
You are no saint,
And you will never be one

Crush

Even when you look at
Your sacrifices
And believe you should be.
Everyone values their happiness
Above everyone else's.
If they didn't,
They wouldn't take so readily
All that you give.
Right now, I sit in limbo,
Between the end and the beginning.
My memories echo silence in the caverns of
My open heart and mind.
There are friends I have not met,
Loves I have not shared
My heart with,
And souls I have not known.
Maybe in the days of
The remainder of my life,
I will find the spirit
I once thought you had;
The spirit who is true
To himself
And lives on his own terms
And for the purpose of himself.
And maybe no such person
Exists.

Jodie Toohey

The Fight

I cannot fight
This battle for you.
It is not mine to fight;
It is yours.
If you value this,
You must value it enough
To fight to keep it.
If you do not value it enough
To fight to keep it,
You will lose it.
I am finished fighting;
Finished fighting for you
To want to keep it;
Finished fighting for you
To hold on to it.
You must now fight
The battle yourself
And if you don't,
I must face the truth.
A battle is never won
Which you never knew
Was there to fight.

Memories And Guesses

Memories and guesses are all I have
Since you went away.
Memories of how we were;
Guessing why you wouldn't stay.

Feeling your lips
Pressing soft on mine.
Wondering what was missing;
What you couldn't find.

Remembering the times
When I'd think of you and smile.
Throwing all the memories
In a sad and lonely pile.

Asking myself
Why did it have to change?
Why, now that you're gone
Does my world seem so strange?

For a long, long time
I'll be remembering you,
And for a long, long time I'll be
Guessing why we are now through.

Jodie Toohey

Divergence

Two different people
From two different worlds,
Departing to opposite ends,
Searching different goals.

But the same smile
That hides the same pain.
The same feeling inside,
Playing the same game.

Paying For Changes

I can't get you out of my mind;
I can't get you out of my heart.
Everything I feel inside
Is tearing me apart.

Sometimes I hate you
Or want to be friends.
I don't know how you feel,
So the confusion never ends.

One day, you were there,
The next, you were gone.
And I need to find out
What exactly went wrong.

It all changed so fast,
Changed just in one day.
I wasn't even there,
So why do I pay?

I don't know what happened;
I don't know what was said,
But because of it, I know
Our romance is dead.

Jodie Toohey

False Starts

We couldn't traverse the anger;
We couldn't navigate the pain.
We never got to see sunshine
After the rain.

We tried to write the novel
But were blocked at the start.
We couldn't persuade words to stay
So the book fell apart.

The words caught in our throats
When we tried to sing the song.
We couldn't find the rhythm;
The melody went wrong.

I'm still standing where you left me,
Drowning in my tears.
I'm realizing I'll be loving you
For many, many years.

Unfulfilled Dreams

I'm tired of dreaming and hunting
For ways to make it right.
I'm tired of thinking and believing
You won't put up a fight.

People say dreams do come true
If you work hard enough
But nobody ever said
It would be this tough.

I thought dreams were to follow
And rules made to break
But my dreams just fall apart,
And my heart breaks.
I dream for you to be with me;
To always be together.
I wish my dream reality
But fear it won't be, ever.

I might as well face fact,
My dream of you won't come true.
I'll resign to live life alone;
There's no more I can do.

People say, "Never give up on love,"
"Dreaming is done for free."
I will foolishly still hope to win your heart,
Until if you fall back in love with me.

Jodie Toohey

Anticipation

I said good-bye as tears
Streamed down angry cheeks.
The pain inside
Was strangling
My spirit
And smothering
My love of life.

I could not live for him
As I refused to ask him
To live for me.

I've let him go to her,
To where I dreamed
deep within
I would always be.

He was mine
But not
What I dreamed at all.
It was obligation
And convention.
It was pressure
And aching need.

Resolutions to stop thinking;
Determination to keep away
Ends with the ring of his call.
The promise of pain's end
Breaks with tears on my pillow.

Giving Without Receiving

I gave you my hand;
I gave you my time.
I gave you my heart,
Is that a crime?

You took what you could
And never gave in return.
You set my heart afire
And left it to burn.

You took my pride,
You took my heart.
You took happy feelings
And ripped them apart.

I gave what you wanted;
The words, the calls and such
You gave me a little
But not very much.

Jodie Toohey

Wonder

I wonder where
Fear is born.
I wonder where
It grows.
I wonder where
Security went.
I wonder what
It knows.
I wonder how
I lost my strength.
I wonder how
I lost my drive.
I wonder when
I'll find belief,
I wonder when
I'll feel alive.

Adolescence

Words fall beneath the sky;
I don't know why I cry.
I kiss the morning dew;
Fall away with thoughts of you.
Faces felt, but never knew.
Your body falls in silence
Through the air
And to the sodden Earth.
Waiting for our birth.
Words that cry out in pain
As we stare at silence slain.
As tears fall in the rain.
Candy kisses, sweet gumdrops
A bomb of pain upon us drops.
Pulling out all the stops.
Fear pulls you toward the moon;
I stare in awe at the ruin,
Singing your lost tune.

Chapter 4
Closure

Jodie Toohey

Memories

Time; I always remember
the times; the age;
the eras of my life,
all folded together
in chronological order
of my world; my story;
my life.

Yesterday

I have a strong desire
To hold your body near.
I have it all in my heart;
The hope, the dream, the fear.

I fear we'll never
Be the friends we used to be.
Fear there will always be a wall between us
And someday you'll be able to see.

That you'll see I really care
And see the pain I feel inside.
That someday you'll miss me
After all my tears have dried.

The tears I cry for your kiss
And the ones that miss your smile.
They I try to keep inside
That sometimes slip out for awhile.

The times when I go through the day
Without seeing your face or hearing your voice.
When I think of you and realize
I no longer have a choice.

The choice of holding your hand close,
Feeling your warm skin soft on mine.

Jodie Toohey

The choice of being all alone
Or deciding to feel fine.

Fine because I saw your smile
And received your loving gaze.
Fine because when I looked into your eyes,
I knew we both treasured the yesterdays.

Yesterdays of calling you on the phone
And at my door you would appear.
Yesterdays of sharing our dreams
And never of losing you I'd fear.

The Second Time
Getting Over You

I'm letting you go again,
But this time you'll go as a friend.
I let go of you once, then came back.
I almost forgot but I got off track.

Before, I couldn't fully let go
Because there still were things I had to know.
I still had the anger, the hurt and the tears
That I know I would have felt the rest of my years.
I'm glad I grabbed onto you again that way
Because I wouldn't have thought how I do today.

I would've never let go and been full of hate.
You wouldn't have come back but I would still wait.
But I came back and I cried the tears.
I let out the anger, asked my questions, and faced
fears.

Even though it took awhile, I got the truth out.
I asked and you told me what you're all about.
Thank you for giving it to me straight.
Your answers to my questions were worth the wait.

Thank you for listening and trying to understand.

Jodie Toohey

Thank you for caring and giving me a hand.
When you told me what you wanted, I didn't get it then,
But later I understood, which ended the confusion.

I don't think you meant to hurt me but you did very much
So when I tried to let go, that was a crutch.
Now, I forgive you for what you might or might not have done.
Since now, I know why you did what you did, I don't need to run.

Maybe we won't be friends on the outside but you will in my heart
And in our hearts, our friendship will never fall apart.
I'll be what you said you wanted because now I want that, too.
But if you ever need me for anything, I hope you'll know what to do.

You come to me if you ever need to talk,
Or down memory lane you want to walk.
Remember and don't forget;
Don't forget anything, remember every bit.

I can really let go now because I understand and forgive
Because of you talking things out with me, I can go on and give.

Crush

If anyone ever asks me about you, this is what I
will say:
"Yes, I know him, great person, great friends we
were, we go back a long way."

Jodie Toohey

Gone But Not Forgotten

Gone but not forgotten;
Your memory lives on.
Time erases the pain
But never breaks the bond.

Gone but not forgotten;
The days you shared with me.
Time hides the love away
And never sets it free.

Gone but not forgotten;
The promises we made.
Time dilutes the vow
And never finds it paid.

Gone but not forgotten;
Your laugh, touch, and smile.
Gone but not forgotten;
Existing for awhile.

Goodbye

I must leave you now
My friend.
My dream awaits.
Do not shed a tear
Or try to hold me back.
Follow your dream;
Embrace it.

Jodie Toohey

Unknown Dreams

Answers I wanted to know
But never did I ask.
Topics we should've discussed
But it seemed like such a task.

Wasted time; lifeless hearts,
Forgotten rhyme; missing parts.

I never wanted to think about
The day you had to go.
Too busy having fun to tell you
The things you wanted to know.

Warm wet cheeks; sad goodbyes,
Emotions meek; lovers' lies.

Fantasies we held in our hearts,
We let our minds believe.
Now after these months have passed
Lost friendship is all we grieve.

Unknown dreams; crazy nights,
Pretty moonbeams; alpine sights.

Trio

There live three memories
All too easy to find.
Relationships with them
Keep reeling in my mind.
Thoughts of them bring
Questions, pain, anger, and fear.
Make me feel sorry they left
And wish they were still here.

One brought desire,
One brought emotion,
And the other was my best friend.
We met in the shadows
And our lips we would lend.

Because of talking and kissing,
We taught each other valuable things.
We learned the art of romance,
And dealt with problems it brings.

Now he's gone and I often wonder
If he knew how I really cared.
Or if he understood
I'll never regret what we shared.

He was only a friend
But soon became much more.
He filled my heart with affection

Jodie Toohey

And started inside me, a war.

I remember how our eyes locked;
And seemed to view each other's soul
Our hands brushed each other's
At every moment we stole.

But neither had the courage
To bring our lips together;
Never ventured to the next step
Faded feelings we held for each other.

When we were just small,
I didn't like him at all,
But somehow when I needed someone
He always answered my call.

We laughed and shared
As only best friends do.
He understood me more
Than anyone else I knew.

He went away for awhile
And returned as someone new,
Inside, he changed
And forgot the friendship we knew.

Though all three losses still bring pain,
And memories frequently cloud my mind,
It's time to hide them safely away
And venture to discover what else I can find.

Never Be Sorry

Never be sorry;
Never be sorry
For time wasted.
Never be sorry
And never cry.
Never forget me
Or feelings inside.

Jodie Toohey

Our Last Night

Some things I never said;
Some things you'll never know.
Things I was afraid to say,
Things I tried to let go.
I don't know if you understood
Things I did or did not say.
I tried to show you I care
And will never regret yesterday.
On that crescent moonlit night
I tried to give you a memory;
Our faces shadowed by the dark;
Hearts beating wildly.
I know you know how I felt
Just as what you felt for me.
I shared my lips with you
And will never be sorry.
Now you've gone so far away;
We're never meant to meet again
But I'll never forget our one shared kiss,
Wherever life takes me, wherever I've been.

Abandon

A distant day far away
calls my name
and beckons me
to abandon;
abandon you,
abandon home;
abandon the me
I used to know.
Abandoned fears,
abandoned dreams
Fall around my feet.
I wave goodbye to you,
no regrets, just pain.

Jodie Toohey

Always

Memories flash like scenes
In movie theater trailers.
I hear your frustrated words,
"I have feelings for you."
Those words just forgotten memories;
Emerging from the deep,
Escaping eternal storage
To here, where we once sat
Together, as friends, practicing love.
We were two lost souls
Looking for our romantic dreams
Led astray in the shuffle of real life.
Romantic dreams evolved into new wishes
That can never be so elusive or fascinating
As the dreams we held
Through our pre-adult years.
You and I have left our homes,
Our naïve juvenile dreams, and each other.
Left only with memories flashing
At extraordinary peaceful moments
And an emotion always
Just beyond consciousness
Assuring wherever I go,
Whatever I do or become
I will always remember with no remorse,
Every moment we shared.

Time

Flies and crawls.
Friend and foe.
Changes everything;
Heals gaping wounds.
Looking glass into tomorrow.
Fades away the sorrow.

Jodie Toohey

Regret

Realizing tomorrow has come.
Knowing what it brought.
Questions asked yesterday
Are answered by today.
If only what is known now
Was known back then.
Wanting to go back in time;
Yearning to take the action now
That produced fear then.
Wasting valuable time;
Looking back instead of around.

Must

I must go on and live;
I must not always cry.
I must learn to freely give;
I mustn't let myself lie.
I must believe in you,
I must believe in me.
I must keep rolling on.
I must simply be.

Jodie Toohey

Memories

Time tallied up
Passes away into
Nothing.
Lost.
A million days
Compressed into a few
Minutes.

Crush

Remember

Remember words,
Remember rhymes.
Remember days,
Remember times.
Remember me
The way I was
When you knew me
To be beautiful
And admirable.
Remember today,
Remember yesterday.
Remember always.
Know I still
Remember you.

Jodie Toohey

Thank You

Thank you for
Drying the tears
As they spilled
From my eyes.
Thank you for
Answering my laughter
With your warm
Amused smiles.
Thank you for
Opening your ears
And your heart
To the words
I'd have to say.
Thank you for
Believing in me
Even when I thought
I lost my way.
Thank you for being
Everything you've been.
Thank you for
What I have found.
Thank you for
Being a friend.

Bonus Poems:
The Crush

Orphan

What you don't see
From far away is
Undeniable, magnified.
My bright colors
A ruse, hiding
In shadows.

If you would see,
You couldn't deny
The melancholy, silent.
Blemishes you must
Accept, flaws
And all the tears fall.

If you would look,
You would act,
Take desperation, longing.
But pleading you won't see,
Will not look
And set me free.

Jodie Toohey

The Relationship

I Walk Here

I walk here
When the snowflakes
Tickle my nose
And pond on my eyelashes.

I walk here when cool wind
Chills my cheeks
And leaves crunch
Under my feet.

I walk here with
Searing heat
And blooming tulips,
Oppressive humidity and
Sun warmed air.

I walk here with a heavy heart,
I walk here with joy.
I walk here buried
In my past and
Clawing for my future.

I walk here under raindrops
And clouds dancing with
Sun rays.

Crush

Under moonlight.
And streetlight.

I walk here with you.

Jodie Toohey

The Goodbye

Let Me In

From a seed deep
In the bottom of
Pool of despair.
Seep upwards in
A trickle then bubbles.
A smoky form floats,
Flirts under doorways
Into dark, cold corners.
From somewhere far behind
Around the mountains
On hand tacked tracks.
A dark rustle in the heat-starved
Weeping willow trees.
Hands above my head in silver clouds
Saturated in seeping down,
Nearly unnoticeably covering me in shame,
Sophisticated sickness swallow
My toes.
Breathe in the quiet, let shoulders settle.
Maybe he left, maybe moved on,
Maybe gone.
Echoes back from yesterday,
Steal tomorrow
Twisted from my sweaty grasp,
Crawling back.

Closure

With Me

I carry you with me
Always.
Every day.
It is a moment, a minute,
Or a crippled afternoon.
A passing thought,
A twist in my gut,
Or a gash in my heart.
It is a butterfly thought,
A wondering,
Or tears of longing.
It is a context of degree
But you are here
With me
Always.
Every day.

ABOUT THE AUTHOR

Jodie Toohey is the author of one additional poetry collection – *Other Side of Crazy* (918studio, 2013) – and two novels – *Missing Emily: Croatian Life Letters* and *Melody Madson – May It Please the Court?* When she's not writing poetry and fiction, she is helping people say what they want to say through her writing and editing company, Wordsy Woman. She lives in Iowa with her husband, teenaged daughter and son, cat, and dog.

Visit Jodie on the web:
www.jodietoohey.com

Want help getting your own book?

Visit my author services website:
www.wordsywomanforauthors.com